Harlow's Journey Home

written by **Ashley Tomassini-Labelle**

◆ FriesenPress

Suite 300 - 990 Fort St
Victoria, BC, V8V 3K2
Canada

www.friesenpress.com

ISBN
978-1-5255-9389-5 (Hardcover)
978-1-5255-9388-8 (Paperback)
978-1-5255-9390-1 (eBook)

1. Juvenile Nonfiction, Animals, Dogs

Distributed to the trade by The Ingram Book Company

Dedication

To all my wonderful nieces and nephews;
I can't wait to read you this story.

To my husband, my best friend; thank you for your constant
love, support and a lifetime of adventure.

And to Helpaws; your selflessness and dedication to these
animals has not gone unnoticed. You have brought joy
to thousands of people because your hearts are so big.
Our homes are all full of a little more love because of you.
"Thank you" hardly seems like enough...this one's for you.

Hi!

I'm Harlow, and this is my journey to find my forever home. My first year has been full of excitement. Let's go back and I'll tell you all about it!

First, let me tell you about my humans. They love to travel and they have been all over the world. On one adventure, they met a bunch of puppies. Some were just like me, and some were completely different.

There were some puppies that were big and tall, and some that were so skinny and so small. These puppies did not have homes to call their own. This made my humans very sad. They knew they had to do something to help, even if they could only help one puppy.

That's where I came in!

I was born on a small island in the Caribbean called St. Lucia
My mom and dad had so many puppies! I had brothers and
sisters of all different colours. Some were tan, some were
black, some were white, and some were brown just like me
No matter what colour we were, we loved each other just
the same!

Over time there were just too many of us to care for. One-by-
one, families came to pick up my brothers and sisters
and bring them to their forever homes. I was starting
to feel really lonely, but I knew in my heart that my
forever family was out there looking for me.

Days passed and weeks went by. Eventually, I was all alone . . . until one special day when Megan showed up and saved me. She seemed really happy that she had found me! If I am being honest, I was relieved that she found me too. We hopped in the car and drove off with the windows down and our faces in the wind.

It was time to start living my life.

Megan brought me t
dog shelter on the is
There were tons of
puppies to play with! I w
excited to make new fri

Charlene came out to greet me. With my tail wagging, I followed her as she showed me around. I found out they called themselves "Helpaws." These girls did everything for us! I now had toys to play with and yummy food to eat. I've never had treats before, but wow, let me tell you, they are delicious!

They gave me plenty of warm baths and helped me get rid of those pesky fleas so I didn't have to scratch so much.

They also gave me medicine to help me grow strong and healthy. It did not take long for me to start feeling better.

I had a new bed to sleep in and my blanket was so soft! I even had a roommate. Her name was Zoe. We spent so many nights cuddling to keep warm and sharing stories. She was my new best friend and we did everything together.

Zoe told me she'd heard a rumour that Charlene and Megan were going to find us our forever homes. From that point on, I made sure to be on my best behaviour. I couldn't wait for someone to love me because I knew

I had so much love to give!

A few months went by and I had not been adopted. I started to wonder if the problem was me.

Was I too small?

Was it the colour of my fur?

Was I getting too old?

How could I stand out?

I dreamed about the day I would be adopted. I wondered what my new family would be like.

Would they be nice?

Would they like to play fetch?

I knew I could find the perfect family, so when it came time for picture day, I made sure to smile extra big!

Then one day the call came.

My humans had picked
ME!

They didn't pick me because I was big or small, or short or tall. They did not care what colour I was at all. When they heard I had been passed over time and time again, they just knew they had to meet me.

Everything started happening so fast. I couldn't wait to tell Zoe that I had found a family. When I got back to our room, we both ran up to each other. We blurted out at the same time:

"I'm getting a family!"

Megan and Charlene had found us both new homes. We were so excited! We could hardly wait to meet our new families. The girls got us all packed up and told us about this place called "Canada" where our new humans lived.

I got to go on my first airplane ride. When the day came, they loaded me into my crate and I boarded the plane.

Everyone at Helpaws had been so good to me. I sure was going to miss them. I grabbed my seat and watched as the girls waved goodbye in the distance. My new life in Canada was about to begin.

The plane ride was a little bumpy because there was a snowstorm outside. I have to admit I was a little nervous. I had never seen snow before.

Once we had landed, there were all these happy humans waiting to greet us. My humans were overjoyed and couldn't stop smiling. They picked me up and hugged me tight. I just knew I was the luckiest puppy in the world.

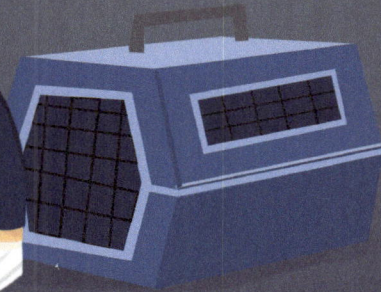

Driving to my new home, I wondered what it would look like. I stared out the window, distracted by all this white stuff floating around. I had never seen anything like it before! When I had left St. Lucia it was sunny and hot. This was going to be my first winter. I was worried Canada would be too cold for me, but I just couldn't wait to jump out of the car and test out the white stuff.

When we pulled up to my new home, my humans put a warm red jacket on me and plopped me right in the snow. At first it was cold, and I was a little scared to move, but once my humans threw that first snowball and I ran to chase it, I realized how fluffy and fun the snow could be!

Now, I love the snow!

I'm in my new home now, and let me tell you, it's better than ever dreamed. I have a big comfy dog bed I can relax on a day. At night, I get to sleep in a huge bed with my humans.

Oh, and the treats! There are so many and they are so good

I have a yard to run around in and lots of trails to go for walks There are even beaches nearby where we can go for swims I feel like I am near the ocean again!

And let me tell you, my humans are so good at playing fetch

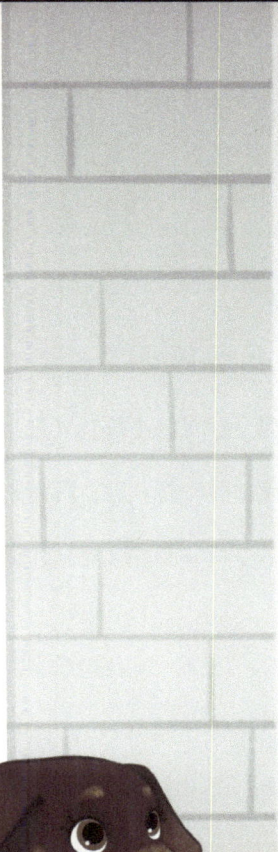

I even have a new brother! His name is Joey. He is shaggy and really small. I have to make sure to play gently with him even though he is older than me, because I am bigger than him. I make sure I always stand up for Joey and protect him.

Joey and I like a lot of the same things, so we get along pretty well. He sure does like to nap, though! I love snuggling up beside him so that he feels safe and knows he is never alone.

To make sure I stay healthy, my humans bring me to the veterinarian regularly. Dr. Lesley checks me out and makes sure I am in tip-top puppy shape.

I always make sure to swing by and visit the girls at the front desk because they have treats. When I am a good girl, they reward me for being on my best behaviour.

Now that I am in my forever home, I have so many new friends of all different shapes and sizes. They are from all over the world! There is Lily the French Bulldog and Finn from the Dominican. I even get to see my old pal, Zoe, because she lives in the same city I do. Every day I feel so lucky to have such a wonderful place to live.

HARLOW

LILY

FINN

ZOE

My humans have already taught me so much. I know how to sit, lay down, and shake a paw, but also how to play nice with others and be kind to everyone I meet. I can't wait to go on more adventures and meet new friends along the way.

Stay tuned, because this story is only just beginning!

About the Author

Harlow's Journey Home is a true story, and Ashley Tomassini-Labelle's first book. She is a world-traveller who has seen her fair share of stray animals. When she met Harlow, she realized that even though she can't save every animal, she could save at least one. She aims to encourage others to help animals in need and consider the adoption of rescues. Ashley looks forward to continuing her travels and lives in Ottawa, Ontario with her family.

CPSIA information can be obtained
at www.ICGtesting.com
Printed in the USA
BVHW021946020821
613478BV00008B/146